☆ 25 Fun and Fabulous ☆
☆ Literature Response ☆
☆ Activities and Rubrics ☆

by Christine Boardman Moen

SCHOLASTIC
PROFESSIONAL BOOKS

NEW YORK • TORONTO • LONDON • AUCKLAND • SYDNEY
MEXICO CITY • NEW DELHI • HONG KONG • BUENOS AIRES

DEDICATION

This book is dedicated to all of my students
who have taught me so much throughout the years.

I especially wish to acknowledge the wonderful students
at Dakota Junior High and my principal, Deb Keith.

Cover design by George Myer
Interior design by Solutions by Design, Inc.

ISBN 0-439-28235-7
Copyright © 2002 by Christine Boardman Moen.
All rights reserved. Printed in the U.S.A.

Table of Contents

About the Book

25 Fun and Fabulous Literature Response Activities and Rubrics is a collection of activities I've developed and used in my classroom since my first book, *Better Than Book Reports*, was published in 1992. Many of the activities focus on the literary elements of character, plot, setting, and theme. Others focus on reading and study skills such as summarizing and note taking. Many activities can be used with fiction and nonfiction books, and several encourage the use of poetry and drama.

All of the activities are extremely flexible. They can be completed by individual students, pairs of students, and students working in small or large groups. Some can be done during the reading of a book and others at the completion of the book. All of the students in your class can do the same activity even if they are reading different books. Conversely, each student may choose a different activity even if the entire class is reading the same book. In addition, I've found that these activities can be applied to any book at any reading level. This ensures that every student in your class—no matter what their reading level—can participate.

Modeling With Short Stories

A unique feature of this book is the inclusion of a list of short stories (or in some cases short novels) that can be used to model the activity.

Using short stories for modeling accomplishes two goals. First, you must read aloud the short story. Reading aloud to students is essential in every classroom and especially important in grades 4–8, when many students begin to devote less time to reading on their own. Secondly, modeling the activity ensures that students will know how to do it on their own.

> **TEACHER NOTE**
> In most cases, you'll need an overhead projector when you model an activity.

Teacher Pages

Each teacher page begins with a brief explanation of the activity. Also included are the activity's objective, a materials listing, and a list of short stories or short novels that are just right for modeling the activity. The suggestions are just that—suggestions. You may prefer to model with stories and novels that you enjoy and are familiar with. At times, you may even want to use students' social studies and science books.

Each teacher page also features a step-by-step guide to modeling the activity as a whole-class activity. Once again, I encourage you to modify any steps to fit your students' learning styles and your own teaching style. The **On Their Own** section tells how students can complete the activity on their own after you've modeled it.

Student Pages

Each reproducible student page briefly describes the activity and gives directions for completing it. Once again, you may want to change some of the directions to fit your students' needs and your instructional goals.

Assessment Rubrics

Each activity is accompanied by an assessment rubric. I give my students the appropriate rubric before they begin their projects so they know how they will be evaluated.

Puzzle Person

Gilly

This activity gives students the opportunity to think carefully about the main character in their book and create a "portrait" of what the character is like on the outside, as well as on the inside. Then they use the portrait to create a Puzzle Person. Each character trait and supporting example is copied onto a puzzle-piece reproducible to create a Puzzle Person.

Modeling the Activity

❋ Read aloud one of the books listed above or any book or story that has a memorable main character. (You could even read a series of picture books that contain a recurring main character, such as Kevin Henkes' delightful Lilly books.)

❋ After each day's reading or after reading an entire short story, ask your students to suggest character traits that describe the main character. Record them on a chart.

❋ Have students find support for their trait choices in the

Objective
Analyze character traits
Materials
For the teacher:
✿ Transparency of page 7
✿ 8 1/2" x 11" drawing of the character you'll use for modeling the activity
For the student:
✿ Copies of pages 7–9
✿ 8 1/2" x 11" sheet of construction paper
✿ Glue, scissors, markers, and colored pencils

Stories for Modeling
Frindle by Andrew Clements (Simon & Schuster, 1996)

Crash by Jerry Spinelli (Knopf, 1996)

Shiloh by Phyllis Reynolds Naylor (Dell, 1991)

book, and add the page numbers of where they found the supporting evidence to the chart.

☀ Once you've completed reading the book or story, review and refine with students the traits and examples listed on the chart.

☀ Place the transparency of the puzzle pieces (page 8) on an overhead projector. Invite students to decide which traits and examples from the chart are the most significant and record these on the different puzzle pieces on the transparency. (Note: While you are writing the character traits on the transparency, have one student copy the examples onto a paper copy of the puzzle pieces.)

☀ Next, glue the construction paper drawing you made ahead of time and the student copy of the puzzle pieces back-to-back. Cut the puzzle pieces apart.

☀ Model how to do a Puzzle Person presentation by reassembling the pieces while reading and explaining each trait and example.

On Their Own

After you've modeled the activity, students can complete it on their own. Provide each student with a copy of pages 7–9, and have them follow the directions on page 7 to create their own Puzzle Person for a book or story they've read.

Puzzle Person

Name_____ Date_____

Story/Book Title_____ Author_____

Main Character_____

Follow these steps to create your Puzzle Person.

1 Identify some character traits of a main character in your book. Some examples of character traits are "honest," "courageous," and "loyal." (Your character may have unattractive traits as well, such as "dishonest" and "bullish.")

2 Page through your book or story and find specific examples that support the different traits you've identified. Record your information on the lines below. Be sure to include the page number to show where you found your example. (If you need more space, continue on the back of the page.)

3 Review your list of traits and examples and choose eight you feel are the best. Record them on the individual pieces on the Puzzle Person Template. Make sure you write in complete sentences and correctly spell all words.

4 Draw a picture of your character on a piece of construction paper. Glue your drawing and the completed Puzzle Person Template together, back-to-back. Cut the puzzle pieces apart.

5 Prepare for your oral presentation by practicing putting the puzzle pieces together while reading and explaining the trait and example on the back of each puzzle piece.

Character Trait	Specific Example(s)	Page Number(s)

Puzzle Person Template

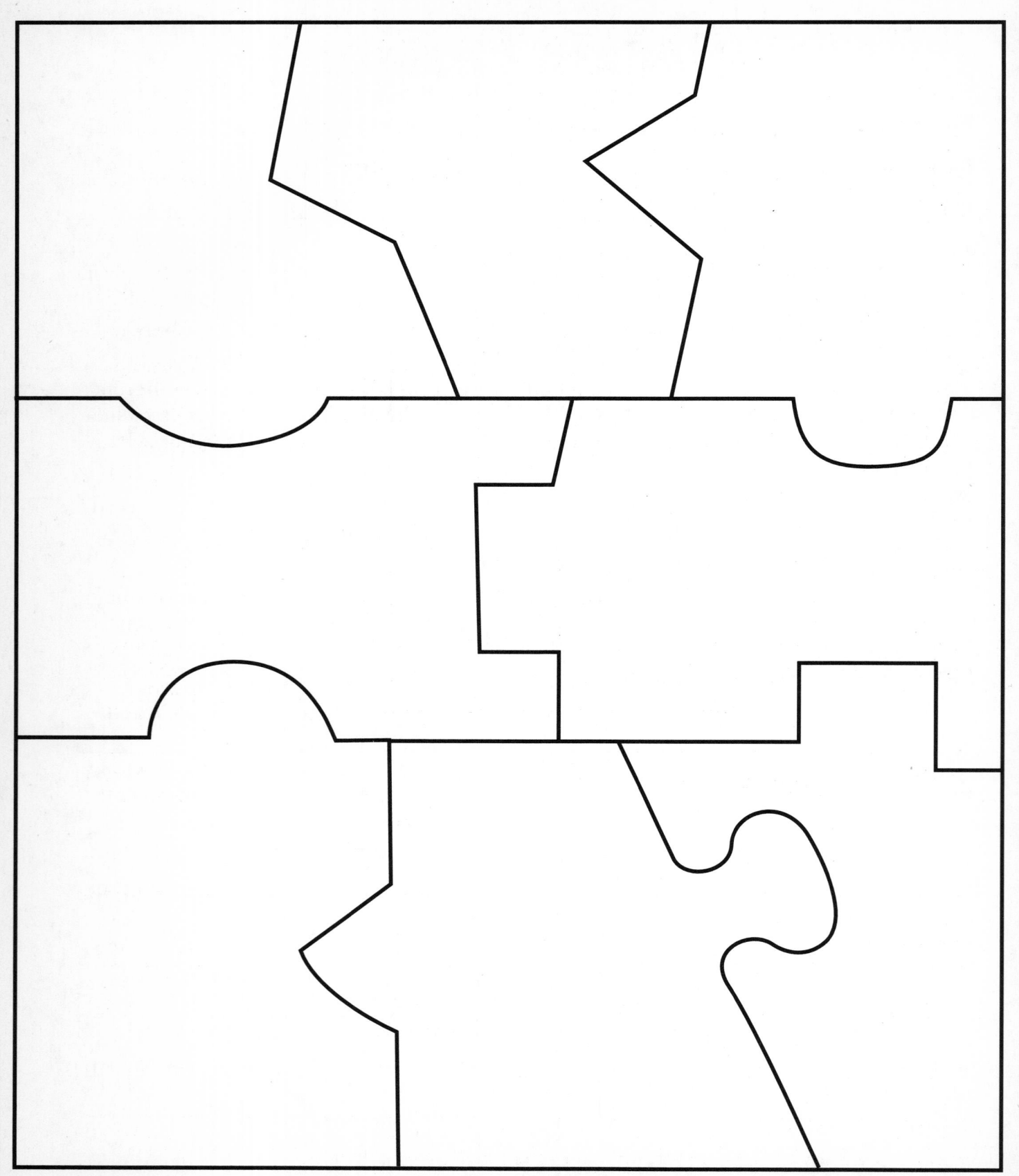

25 Fun and Fabulous Literature Response Activities and Rubrics
Scholastic Professional Books

Puzzle Person

Name _____ Date _____

Story/Book Title _____

Author _____

Main Character_____

Category	Excellent	Above Average	Average	Below Average
Character traits and support examples	Very insightful traits and detailed support examples	Significant traits and good support examples	Good traits and support examples	Missing traits and/or support examples
Character image	Very detailed and very well executed	Detailed and well done	Complete, but lacks some detail	Incomplete and sloppy
Oral presentation	Exceptional; spoke clearly, excellent volume, eye contact, pacing	Well prepared; spoke clearly, good volume, eye contact, pacing	Organized; needs to improve volume and pacing	Disorganized; poor volume, eye contact, and pacing
Effort	Outstanding; used time well	Very good; used time well	Good but needed assistance	Poor; resisted task

Teacher's Comments: _____

_____

_____

_____

_____

Now That I'm Wiser

Objective

Assess character development

Materials

For the teacher:

✤ Transparency of page 12

For the student:

✤ Copies of pages 12 and 13

Stories for Modeling

"A Matter of Getting Out" by Lois Duncan et al. from *Trapped! Cages of Mind & Body* (Aladdin Paperbacks, 1999)

The Library Card by Jerry Spinelli (Scholastic, 1997)

The Talking Earth by Jean Craighead George (Harper, 1987)

When I was younger,

I went to Mt. Rushmore. When I looked up at the monument, I said, "Hey that's Aberlinchonham!"

My mom's friend Tonya gave me a Blacklab puppy for my 4th Birthday, and we named him Shane.

We moved into a new house, and Because I thought my mom and Dad would leave me, I slept with The keys in my pjs.

When I was younger, I believed in Santa Clause.

Now that I'm older, I

  Go everywhere I can.

   Listen more.

    Spend more time with my grandma and grandpa.

Now that I'm older, I believe that Santa Clause is my mom and dad.

Amy

Often story characters, like people in real life, change and grow in wisdom as a result of life experiences. In this activity, students write a poem to help them explore how a character has changed.

Modeling the Activity

✻ To introduce the idea of change and developing wisdom, I share with my students the following poem I wrote:

When I was younger, I

    sang songs as loudly as I could because
    singing made me feel good.

    loved root beer and my cat Happy
    who got lost when we moved to the city.

    wanted to be me
    but still be like everybody else.

When I was younger, I believed I had all the time in the
world.

Now that I'm older, I

    hum when I don't know the words.
    love root beer and my dog named Buttercup

    want my daughter to be herself and not like
      everybody else.
Now that I'm older, I believe that time is precious and
  priceless.

After reading the poem, have students describe some of
the changes they can infer from the poem.

☀ Have students use page 12 to write their own "When I was
younger, now that I'm wiser." Students who wish to share
their examples are encouraged to do so. (Some examples
can be delightful. One student claimed she believed
leprechauns lived in the tank of her toilet, and since she'd
grown older she didn't believe that anymore—but she
claims she still gets a little nervous around St. Patrick's Day!)

☀ Once students are aware of some of their own changes, they
can apply this awareness to the characters in their stories.
Read aloud the story you chose for modeling the activity. As
a group, have students supply the information for the
"When I was younger, now that I'm wiser" chart as you
record them on the transparency of page 12. Then write a
poem in the format of the poem you shared with them.

On Their Own

Post a sample poem on the board. Give students copies of
pages 12 and 13. Remind students to complete page 12 before
they write their poems. Suggest that students read their
poems aloud so they can hear the rhythm of the language.

> **TEACHER TIP**
>
> Write the under-
> scored lines of the
> poem on the
> chalkboard or on
> chart paper. Explain
> to students that
> they'll use this
> "frame" to write
> their own poems.

Now That I'm Wiser

Name_____ Date_____

Story/Book Title _____

Author _____

Character's Name _____

Complete the chart below to show how a character in your story has grown. Record what the character was like at the beginning of the story under the category "When I Was Younger," and record the changes that occurred in the character during or at the end of the story under "Now That I'm Wiser."

When I Was Younger	Now That I'm Wiser
① _____	_____
_____	_____
② _____	_____
_____	_____
③ _____	_____
_____	_____
④ _____	_____
_____	_____
⑤ _____	_____
_____	_____
⑥ _____	_____
_____	_____

25 Fun and Fabulous Literature Response Activities and Rubrics
Scholastic Professional Books

Now That I'm Wiser

Name_____ Date_____

Story/Book Title _____

Author _____

Category	Excellent	Above Average	Average	Below Average
Followed the poem format	Followed poem format precisely	Slightly varied format	Varied format	Did not follow the format
Word choice	Dynamic word choice	Outstanding word choice	Appropriate word choice	Awkward word choice
Examples of younger and wiser	Unique; insightful	Clever; significant	Good; appropriate	Poor or incomplete
Mechanics (grammar, punctuation, spelling, and capitalization)	Skillful use of mechanics	Very few errors in mechanics	A few errors in mechanics	Several errors in mechanics

Teacher's Comments: _____

_____

_____

_____

_____

_____

Plot Turning Point Posters

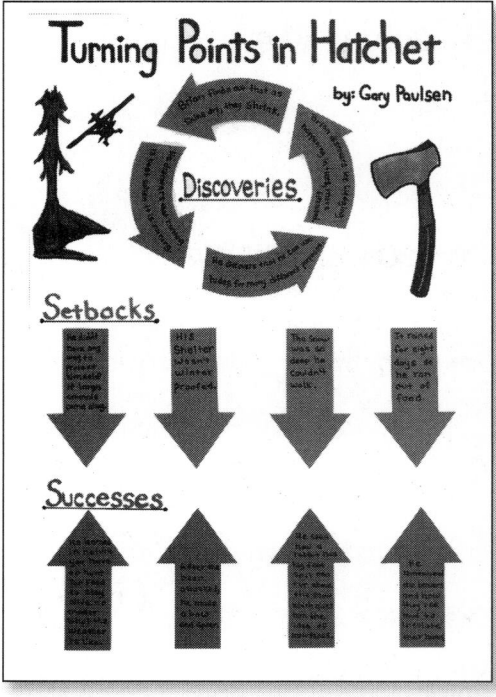

Objective

Categorize plot turning points as discoveries, setbacks, or successes for a character

Materials

For the teacher:

❋ Transparency of page 16

For the student:

❋ Copies of pages 15–17
❋ Posterboard
❋ Scissors, markers, glue
❋ Colored construction paper

Stories for Modeling

Because of Winn-Dixie by Kate DiCamillo (Candlewick Press, 2000)

Riding Freedom by Pam Munoz Ryan (Scholastic, 1998)

Stone Fox by John Reynolds Gardiner (HarperCollins, 1980)

Creating Plot Turning Point Posters helps students explore plot and dig deeply into the minds and motives of the main characters in the stories they read.

Modeling the Activity

❋ Choose a story to use for modeling the activity. Before you begin reading it aloud, tell students to listen carefully for the main character's discoveries, setbacks, and successes.

❋ Provide each student with a copy of page 15. Give them time to complete it. Then have them form pairs to discuss and combine their lists. Have one member from each pair share the three best ideas for each of the three categories.

❋ As students read their best ideas, record the ideas on the board or chart paper. Once the list is complete, the class votes on each idea with a thumbs-up or a thumbs-down sign. Write the three best ideas for each category in the arrows on the transparency of page 16. Tell students the arrows can be cut out to create a poster.

On Their Own

In addition to poster-making supplies (see Materials), provide each student with copies of pages 15–17. Tell students they should be prepared to turn in page 15 so you can see how they categorized the various turning points.

Plot Turning Point Posters

Name_____ Date_____

Story/Book Title _____

Author _____

List the turning points that occurred in the story you read.

DISCOVERIES: What turning points involved your character making a discovery about him or herself?

_____

_____

_____

_____

_____

SETBACKS: What turning points resulted from a setback, challenge, or disappointment your character encountered?

_____

_____

_____

_____

_____

SUCCESSES: What turning points took place because of a success, big or small, that your character experienced?

_____

_____

_____

_____

_____

Plot Turning Point Posters

(continued)

Name_____ Date_____

Story/Book Title _____

Author _____

Reread your list of discoveries, set backs, and successes. Choose the best ones and record them in the appropriate arrows below. Cut out the arrows and use them to create your poster.

Discoveries

Setbacks

Successes

25 Fun and Fabulous Literature Response Activities and Rubrics
Scholastic Professional Books

Plot Turning Point Posters

Name_____   Date_____

Story/Book Title _____

Author _____

Category	Excellent	Above Average	Average	Below Average
Completeness of listed ideas	All items completed	All items completed	One item missing	More than one item missing
Significance of turning points listed	All special and/or stupendous	Almost all special and/or stupendous	Most special	Few special
Clarity of examples	Clearly focused; completely understandable	Clear meaning throughout	At times a bit confusing	Unclear in many instances
Examples in correct categories	All in correct categories	All in correct categories	Most in correct categories	Few in correct categories

Teacher's Comments: _____

_____

_____

_____

_____

_____

_____

_____

Character Ties

Objective

Explore character

Materials

For the teacher:

- Transparency of page 19

For the student:

- Copies of pages 19 and 20
- Poster board
- Newsprint
- Glue, scissors, markers
- Construction paper
- Tie pattern (optional)

Stories for Modeling

"Priscilla and the Wimps" by Richard Peck from *Sixteen Short Stories* by Outstanding Writers for Young Adults (Bantam, 1984)

"Shotgun Cheatham's Last Night Above Ground" by Richard Peck from *A Long Way from Chicago* (Dial Books, 1998)

Mick Harte Was Here by Barbara Park (Scholastic, 1995)

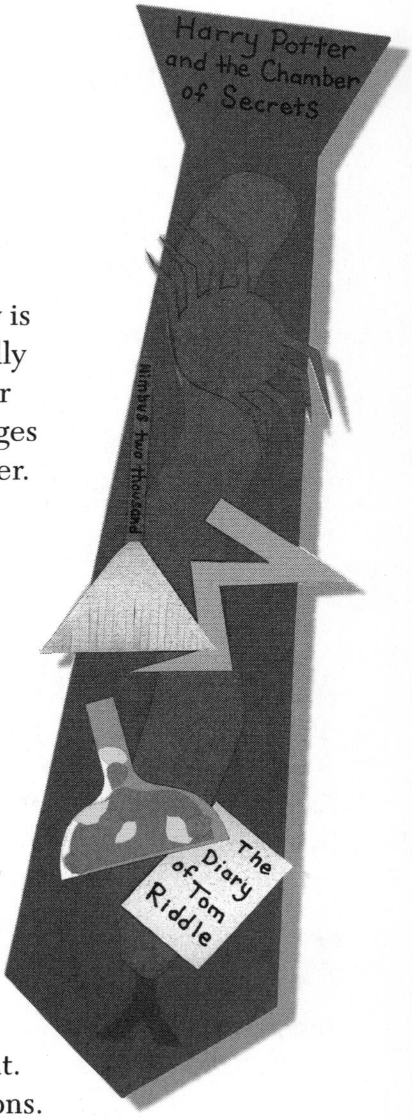

The purpose of this fun activity is to help students think carefully about the character(s) in their books and to create neckties with images that are representative of that character.

Modeling the Activity

- After you've read the story aloud to students, complete Part 1 of the transparency of page 19 together as a class.
- Ask students to suggest symbols that might represent the things they included on their lists. Complete Part 2 of the transparency. As students complete their sample tie illustration on page 19, sketch a tie on the board, or some newsprint. Incorporate the students' suggestions. Have students in small groups share their illustrations and tell the significance of each item.

On Their Own

Students will need copies of pages 19 and 20, as well as tie-making supplies (see Materials). Tell students they should fill out and hand in page 19 with their completed ties so you can use it in your evaluation. After they've finished their ties, students can give a brief oral presentation explaining the significance of the images they included.

Character Ties

Name_____ Date_____

Story/Book Title _____

Author _____

Name of Character _____

1. List six significant things about your character below. These can include the character's personality traits, likes and dislikes, fears, ambitions, friends, family, hobbies, or relationships. Be sure to include the page number to indicate the source of your information.

Character Description	Example/Support Page Number
① _____	
② _____	
③ _____	
④ _____	
⑤ _____	
⑥ _____	

2. Think about images or symbols you might include on your tie to suggest the things on your list. Use the tie outline below to plan your final tie.

Items to be Illustrated		Sample Illustration
① _____	④ _____	
② _____	⑤ _____	
③ _____	⑥ _____	

Character Ties

Name_____ Date_____

Story/Book Title _____

Author _____

Name of Character _____

Category	Excellent	Above Average	Average	Below Average
Character description	Detailed, insightful examples	Detailed, significant examples	Appropriate examples; some detail	General examples; not detailed
Support examples	Each related directly to character trait	Well thought-out examples	Appropriate examples	Poor examples
Number of images	4–6 images	4 images	4 images	Less than 4 images
Appearance of tie	Eye-catching; excellent detail	Attractive; very good detail	Neat; some detail	Sloppy; incomplete

Teacher's Comments: _____

_____

_____

_____

_____

_____

_____

25 Fun and Fabulous Literature Response Activities and Rubrics
Scholastic Professional Books

WHO said WHAT and WHY
(Is It Important?)

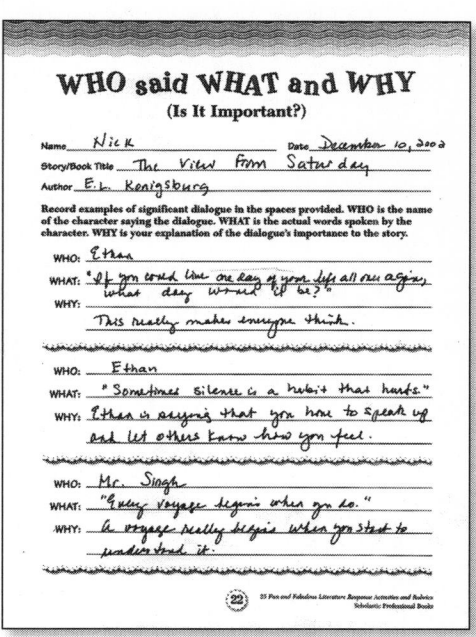

T he WHO said WHAT and WHY (Is It Important?) activity will help students become more aware of significant dialogue. This, in turn, can help them become more sophisticated readers.

Modeling the Activity

✷ Begin by reading aloud several quotations your students may know. Ask students to guess who said the famous words and explain why they are important. For example:

> Mirror, mirror on the wall, who is fairest of us all? (*Snow White's stepmother*)

> …One small step for man, one giant leap for mankind. (*Neil Armstrong*)

> Then I'll huff and I'll puff and I'll blow your house in! (*Big Bad Wolf*)

✷ Read aloud the story you've chosen for modeling the activity. Ask students to identify important pieces of dialogue and explain why they are important to the story. As they do, record their ideas on the overhead transparency of page 22.

✷ After discussing the importance of the dialogue students have suggested, they'll be ready to complete this activity on their own.

On Their Own

Provide students with copies of pages 22 and 23. Suggest that as they read their book, they use sticky-notes to mark pages where they think a character has said something especially important. Then students can follow the directions to fill in page 22.

Objective
Evaluate dialogue and explain its significance

Materials
For the teacher:
✷ Transparency of page 22

For the student:
✷ Copies of pages 22 and 23

Stories for Modeling
"Baseball in April" by Gary Soto from *Baseball in April and Other Stories* (Harcourt, 1990)

"The Original Recipe" by Michael Dorris from *Help Wanted* (Little, Brown, 1997)

WHO said WHAT and WHY
(Is It Important?)

Name_____   Date_____

Story/Book Title _____

Author _____

Record examples of significant dialogue in the spaces provided. WHO is the name of the character saying the dialogue. WHAT is the actual words spoken by the character. WHY is your explanation of the dialogue's importance to the story.

WHO: _____

WHAT: _____

WHY: _____

_____

WHO: _____

WHAT: _____

WHY: _____

_____

WHO: _____

WHAT: _____

WHY: _____

_____

25 Fun and Fabulous Literature Response Activities and Rubrics
Scholastic Professional Books

WHO said WHAT and WHY
(Is It Important?)

Name_____ Date_____

Story/Book Title _____

Author _____

Category	Excellent	Above Average	Average	Below Average
Significance of examples of dialogue	Most vital dialogue in book	Significant dialogue	Somewhat significant dialogue	Unimportant dialogue from book
Clarity of explanation	Clearly focused; completely understandable	Clear meaning throughout	At times a bit confusing	Confusing in many places
Number of items completed	All items completed	All items completed	One item missing	More than one item missing
Mechanics (grammar, punctuation, spelling, and capitalization)	Skillful use of mechanics	Very few errors in mechanics	A few errors in mechanics	Several errors in mechanics

Teacher's Comments: _____

_____

_____

_____

_____

_____

Tampering With Titles

Objective

Evaluate story titles

Materials

For the teacher:

☀ Transparency of page 25

☀ Summary of a book students are unfamiliar with

For the student:

☀ Copies of page 25 and 26

Stories for Modeling

Burger Wuss by M. T. Anderson et al. (Candlewick Press, 1999)

Frindle by Andrew Clements (Simon & Schuster, 1996)

The Power of Un by Nancy Etchemendy (Front Street/Cricket Books, 2000)

A book's title is one of the first things a student looks at and can determine whether the student will read the book. In this activity, students analyze and evaluate book titles.

Tampering With Titles

Name: Magdely   Date: 1/10/03
Story/Book Title: The Giver
Author: Lois Lowry

Think carefully about your story or book and its title and then complete each section below.

Give several specific reasons why the title of your story/book should or should not be changed.

Jonas is being trained to become the Giver so I think the title is a good one. Also the current Giver is such an important character and an important person in the world Jonas lives in.

Create a logical alternative to your story/book's title. Explain why the new title is appropriate.

The Receiver. This title could work because Jonas never actually becomes the Giver.

Create an illogical or opposite title for your story/book. Explain why the new title is not appropriate.

The Good Society. This title wouldn't work because the society Jonas lives in is really evil.

25 Fun and Fabulous Literature Response Activities and Rubrics
Scholastic Professional Books   **25**

Modeling the Activity

☀ Introduce your students to this activity by reading the summary of a book to them—a book they wouldn't be familiar with. Ask students to suggest titles for the book based on the summary. Then show them the book cover.

☀ Next, show students a book they are familiar with. Ask students to create alternative titles for the book. Record them on the board. Ask students if they agree or disagree that an alternative title can be as effective as the published title. As a class, complete the transparency of page 25. Encourage students to explain their answers.

On Their Own

Provide students with copies of pages 25 and 26. Allow time for students to share and discuss their "Tampered Titles."

Tampering With Titles

Name_____ Date_____

Story/Book Title _____

Author _____

Think carefully about your story or book and its title, then complete each section below. Use the back of this sheet if you need more room.

Give several specific reasons why the title of your story/book should or should not be changed.

_____

_____

_____

_____

_____

_____

_____

_____

Create a logical alternative to your story/book's title. Explain why the new title is appropriate.

_____

_____

_____

Create an illogical or opposite title for your story/book. Explain why the new title is not appropriate.

_____

_____

_____

Tampering With Titles

Name_____   Date_____

Story/Book Title _____

Author _____

Category	Excellent	Above Average	Average	Below Average
Reasons given for titles	Insightful; all specific	Thoughtful; most specific	Appropriate; general	Poor quality; few given
Word choice	Dynamic word choice	Outstanding word choice	Appropriate word choice	Awkward word choice
Creativity of titles and ideas	Insightful	Clever	Appropriate	Unoriginal
Mechanics (grammar, punctuation, spelling, and capitalization)	Skillful use of mechanics	Very few errors in mechanics	A few errors in mechanics	Several errors in mechanics

Teacher's Comments: _____

_____

_____

_____

_____

_____

_____

_____

Title-Down Paragraphs

Most students are familiar with acrostics. The Title-Down Paragraphs activity utilizes the basic acrostic format to help students build an organized collection of important facts they find in a nonfiction story or book.

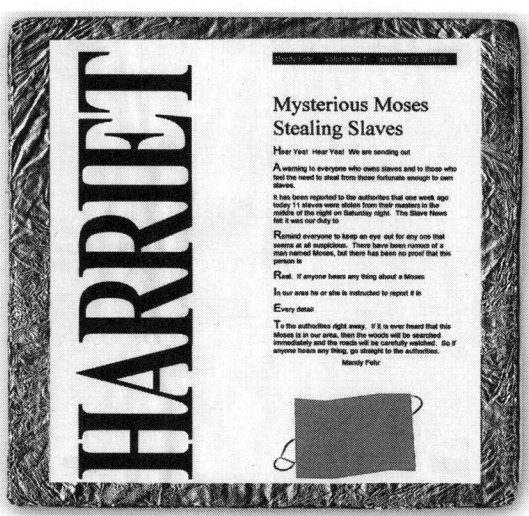

Objective
Select significant facts found in nonfiction text

Materials
For the teacher:
* Transparency of page 28

For the student:
* Copies of pages 28 and 29

Stories for Modeling
Powwow by George Ancona (Harcourt Trade Publishers, 1993)

Kids at Work: Lewis Hine and the Crusade Against Child Labor by Russell Freedman (Clarion, 1994)

The Great Fire by Jim Murphy (Scholastic, 1995)

Modeling the Activity

* Choose a nonfiction story for modeling this activity. After you've read it aloud to your students, ask them to supply a main topic heading for the selection. (A sample is provided on the reproducible on page 28.)

* Record the heading by writing it in bold letters down the left-hand side of the transparency of page 28. Have students generate sentences that provide topic information and record the informational sentences next to the bold letters. (Remind students that their sentences may flow into the next letter in the topic word.)

* Be sure students understand that topics may be identified in different ways. For example, "GREAT FIRE" or "CHICAGO FIRE" would both work for Jim Murphy's book.

On Their Own

Provide students with copies of pages 28 and 29. Students may want to rewrite their Title-Down Paragraphs on a sheet of drawing paper and use creative lettering for the title. Tell students to be prepared to turn in page 28 with their completed paragraphs.

Title-Down Paragraphs

Name_____ Date_____

A Title-Down Paragraph uses an acrostic topic heading to help you organize information you've learned about your topic. Below is a sample Title-Down Paragraph based on information about Harriet Tubman.

MOSES

Moses, or Harriet Tubman, was the most famous conductor on the Underground Railroad.

Other people who helped Harriet include Thomas Garret of Wilmington, Delaware, and Reverend J. W. Loguen of Syracuse, New York.

Saying the phrase, "A friend with friends," indicated Harriet was waiting outside a "safehouse" with runaway slaves.

Even Harriet was scared sometimes, and she knew she had to carry a gun, because once a

Slave ran away, he or she could never return to the plantation for fear of being forced to tell the names and places of the people involved in the Underground Railroad.

Plan your Title-Down Paragraph by filling in the information below. Use the back of this sheet if you need more room. When you have rewritten and edited your paragraph, copy it onto a separate sheet of paper.

Possible Topic Title_____ _____ _____

Topic Letters	Sentences of Fact

25 Fun and Fabulous Literature Response Activities and Rubrics
Scholastic Professional Books

Title-Down Paragraphs

Name_____ Date_____

Topic Title _____

Source of Information _____

Category	Excellent	Above Average	Average	Below Average
Topic title/ choice	Insightful; fits the most important facts	Creative; fits the facts	Appropriate; fits most facts	Inaccurate; misses main idea
Sentences	Varied, complete sentences	Complete sentences; good details	Complete sentences	Incomplete sentences
Mechanics	Skillful use of mechanics	Very few errors in mechanics	A few errors in mechanics	Several errors in mechanics
Appearance	Eye-catching	Attractive	Neat	Sloppy
Accuracy of facts	Completely accurate	Completely accurate	Mostly accurate	Somewhat accurate

Teacher's Comments: _____

_____

_____

_____

_____

_____

_____

Telephone Talk

Objective
Assess characters' emotions
Materials
For the teacher:
* Transparency of page 32
* Pair of dice
For the student:
* Copies of pages 32 and 33
* Paper

Stories for Modeling
"The Truth About Sharks" by Joan Bauer from *One Experience to Another* (Tom Doherty Associates, 1997)

"Final Cut" by Rich Wallace from *Lost and Found* (Tom Doherty Associates, 2000)

"Victor" by James Howe from *Birthday Surprises: Ten Great Stories to Unwrap* (Beech Tree, 1995)

A student's reading experience is enhanced when she or he identifies with a book's character or relates to the story's events in some way. The Telephone Talk activity helps students relate to a character's emotions.

Modeling the Activity

✷ Ask students to list five emotions on the left side of a blank sheet of paper. Then ask them to reflect quietly about times when they've experienced those emotions. Have them briefly identify the time, place, and circumstance for each and add this information in the right column.

✷ Have students rank the emotional experiences from 1 to 5, with 1 being the most memorable or significant.

✷ Tell students to write their telephone number (or any telephone number) down the left side of another sheet of paper.

✷ Tell students they will write about their most memorable experience. Explain that they are to write using only the number of words in each line as indicated by the telephone number. (A zero is like a wild card—it allows students to use any number of words they wish.)

✳ Give students individual feedback. Decide if you wish to collect the poems and read some aloud with student permission. (I ask students privately while I'm circulating the room if I can share their poems. I use names only if they give me permission.)

✳ After all of your students have completed their telephone poems, read aloud one of the stories listed (see Stories for Modeling) or one of your choosing. As a class, write a telephone poem about a character in the story by following the directions on the transparency of page 32.

On Their Own

Provide students with copies of pages 32 and 33 . If students have read the same story or book, they may enjoy working in pairs. Invite volunteers to read their poems aloud to the class.

TEACHER TIP
Because of the personal nature of this activity, I don't require students to write their names on their papers unless they wish to do so.

Telephone Talk

Name_____ Date_____

Story/Book Title _____

Author _____

Think carefully about the different emotions your main character experienced during the story, and the events that caused these emotions. Identify and describe those emotions and events below. Use descriptive words.

Character's Emotions ⟶ L I N K E D T O ⟶ Story's Events

① _____

② _____

③ _____

④ _____

⑤ _____

Write a 7-digit telephone number in the left-hand column. Using ideas from above, write a poem about the character's emotions on the lines provided. The number of words you write for each line of poetry must match the number on the left.

Number	Poem
_____	_____
_____	_____
_____	_____
_____	_____
_____	_____
_____	_____
_____	_____

25 Fun and Fabulous Literature Response Activities and Rubrics
Scholastic Professional Books

Telephone Talk

Name_____   Date_____

Story/Book Title _____

Author _____

Category	Excellent	Above Average	Average	Below Average
Word choice	Dynamic word choice	Outstanding word choice	Appropriate word choice	Awkward word choice
Accuracy of word count	Used correct number of words	Used correct number of words	Used almost exact number of words	Very noticeable inaccuracy
Creativity	Insightful	Clever	Typical	Unoriginal
Mechanics (punctuation, grammar, spelling, and capitalization)	Skillful use of mechanics	Very few errors in mechanics	A few errors in mechanics	Several errors in mechanics

Teacher's Comments: _____

_____

_____

_____

_____

_____

_____

Sizing Up the Setting

Objective

Compare and contrast story settings

Materials

For the teacher:

- Transparency of page 35
- Blank transparency

For the student:

- Copies of pages 35 and 36
- Markers, colored pencils

Stories for Modeling

The Whipping Boy by Sid Fleischman (Greenwillow, 1986)

Sarah, Plain and Tall by Patricia MacLachlan (HarperCollins, 1995)

Number the Stars by Lois Lowry (Houghton, 1989)

The setting of a story is more than just when and where a story takes place. This activity helps students look more carefully at the setting of a story. They'll think about the lifestyle of the characters, their jobs, family life, wealth, and outlook on life. Illustrating the setting after analyzing it will deepen the understanding of this literary element.

Modeling the Activity

- Tell students they are going to create two different stories about two characters, a girl and a boy, who are their own age. At the top of a blank transparency, write the headings Story A and Story B. Under each heading, list the place, time, family situation, and family income for each story.
- Have students supply a simple plot for each story. (This can be done verbally.) Next, have students compare and contrast the two stories by explaining the effect the setting has on each story even though each story has a common denominator: a girl and boy who are the students' age.
- Finally, read aloud a book or story in which the setting is very important such as those suggested above. After you've completed your read-aloud, complete the top part of the transparency of page 35 as a class.
- Provide students with copies of page 35 and have them complete the bottom half individually. Give students an opportunity to share and discuss their setting drawings.

On Their Own

Students will need copies of pages 35 and 36. Some students may prefer to make larger drawings on a separate sheet of paper. Encourage students to share and explain their drawings.

Sizing Up the Setting

Name_____ Date_____

Story/Book Title _____

Author _____

List important setting elements from your story below. Be sure to include the page number from your book that shows where you found your information.

Setting Elements	Support From Book, Including Page Number
_____	_____
_____	_____
_____	_____
_____	_____

Draw your favorite scene from the book in the space provided. Then answer the questions below.

This scene is where _____

_____.

It's my favorite scene because _____

_____.

Sizing Up the Setting

Name_____   Date_____

Story/Book Title _____

Author_____

Category	Excellent	Above Average	Average	Below Average
Knowledge of story	Insightful	Substantial	Familiar	Little understanding
Clarity of explanations	Clearly focused; completely understandable	Clear meaning throughout	At times a bit confusing	Confusing in many places
Quantity of answers	All answers provided	All answers provided	One answer missing	Few answers provided
Word choice	Dynamic word choice	Outstanding word choice	Appropriate word choice	Awkward word choice

Teacher's Comments: _____

_____

_____

_____

_____

_____

_____

_____

Double-Nickel Stories

Double-Nickel Stories can be used in two significant ways. First, the 55-word story frame can be used to teach students how to write compact stories where—just as in poetry—every word counts. More importantly, however, the 55-word story is an excellent way to check students' reading comprehension.

Modeling the Activity

✸ To help your students better utilize this activity, you may want to have your students generate their own original 55-word stories. To do this, use the SWBS method. SWBS stands for Somebody Wants But So, which are the basic elements of most stories. *Somebody* (the main character) *Wants* something *But* something gets in his or her way (the conflict) *So* the main character solves the problem to get what he or she wants (the resolution).

    Somebody: The three little pigs
      Wants: To live happily ever after
        But: The big, bad wolf tries to eat them
        So: When the wolf comes down the chimney, the pigs make wolf stew

With a little practice, students usually manage to create interesting, often funny, stories with witty dialogue and surprise endings.

✸ Read aloud the story you've chosen to use for modeling the activity. As a group, write a Double-Nickel story following the directions on the transparency of page 38.

On Their Own

Provide students with copies of pages 38 and 39. Encourage volunteers to share their summaries with the class.

Double-Nickel Stories

Name _Audrey_   Date _Sept. 16, 2003_
Story/Book Title _A Wrinkle in Time_
Author _Madeleine L'Engle_

Write a summary of your story using **EXACTLY 55 words.** Here are some suggestions: 1) Use pencil so you can erase. 2) Use characters' names to avoid confusion. 3) Write in complete sentences. 4) Use a variety of sentence types. 5) Write several rough drafts and choose the best sentences and phrases to use in your final draft.

Meg Murray's father has been missing for a year. Mrs. Whatsit shows up, and takes Meg, her brother, and their friend Calvin in a tessering to the planet Uriel. They find their father, encounter the evil IT. Meg must save her brother from IT. She finally rescues him. Her family has a very joyous reunion. **THE END.**

(38) *25 Fun and Fabulous Literature Response Activities and Rubrics*
Scholastic Professional Books

Objective

Summarize a story

Materials

For the teacher:
✿ Transparency of page 38

For the student:
✿ Copies of pages 38 and 39

Stories for Modeling

"My Brother's Keeper" by Jay Bennett from *From One Experience to Another* (Tom Doherty Associates, 1997)

"Who Waxed Mad Max?" by Gary L. Blackwood from *But That's Another Story* (Walker and Company, 1996)

Double-Nickel Stories

Name_____ Date_____

Story/Book Title _____

Author _____

Write a summary of your story using *exactly* 55 words. Here are some suggestions: 1) Use pencil so you can erase; 2) Use characters' names to avoid confusion; 3) Write in complete sentences; 4) Use a variety of sentence types; 5) Write several rough drafts and choose the best sentences and phrases to use in your final summary.

_____ _____ _____ _____ _____ _____

_____ _____ _____ _____ _____ _____

_____ _____ _____ _____ _____ _____

_____ _____ _____ _____ _____ _____

_____ _____ _____ _____ _____ _____

_____ _____ _____ _____ _____ _____

_____ _____ _____ _____ _____ _____

_____ _____ _____ _____ _____ _____

_____ .

25 Fun and Fabulous Literature Response Activities and Rubrics
Scholastic Professional Books

Double-Nickel Stories

Name_____   Date_____

Story/Book Title _____

Author _____

Category	Excellent	Above Average	Average	Below Average
Word choice	Dynamic word choice	Outstanding word choice	Appropriate word choice	Awkward word choice
Sentence variety and completeness	Variety of sentences; complete	Some variety of sentences; complete	No variety; complete sentences	Incomplete
Clarity of meaning	Clearly focused; completely understandable	Clear meaning throughout	At times a bit confusing	Incoherent in many places
Mechanics (Punctuation, spelling, grammar, and capitalization	Skillful use of mechanics	Very few errors in mechanics	A few errors in mechanics	Several errors in mechanics

Teacher's Comments: _____

_____

_____

_____

_____

_____

_____

K-W-Cornell

K-W-Cornell

Name _Anthony_   Date _3/27/02_

Story/Book/Article Title _Immigrant Kids_

Author _Russell Freedman_

Before you read, complete the K and W portions of this page. As you read, stop at the end of each page, section, or chapter of your book and record any main ideas, facts, statistics, examples, or quotations that you find interesting and informative in the Cornell section. Take special note of any information that confirms the ideas you listed under the "K" column or any information that answers questions you wrote under your "W" column.

K (Tell what you KNOW already about this topic.)	W (Tell what you WANT to learn about this topic.)
1. An immigrant comes from another county.	1. What countries did they come from?
2. Many came through Ellis Island.	2. How did they learn English?
3. They spoke different language.	3. What kind of jobs did they get?
4. Most came on ships.	

CORNELL (Main idea, facts, and examples)	Page Number(s)
1. Many immigrants came — 23 million between 1880 - 1920	p. 4
2. Schools — In some schools kids spent 4-5 months learning English.	p. 29
3. Sweatshops — Many kids worked in sweatshops — small apartments turned into factories.	p. 45

25 Fun and Fabulous Literature Response Activities and Rubrics
Scholastic Professional Books   **41**

Rick Prestley, a fellow educator and effective reading education advocate, shared his K-W-Cornell idea at a presentation at the March, 2000, Illinois Reading Conference.

K-W-Cornell is a hybrid of the standard K-W-L chart, which is used in many elementary schools, and the Cornell Method of note taking, which is used in many high school and college classrooms. K-W-Cornell, or this "simple idea" as Rick calls it, can yield sophisticated learning results.

Objective

Apply note-taking strategies to nonfiction text

Materials

For the teacher:

✹ Transparency of page 41

For the student:

✹ Copies of pages 41 and 42

Stories for Modeling

Lincoln: A Photobiography by Russell Freedman (Clarion Books, 1987)

Indian Chiefs by Russell Freedman (Scholastic, 1987)

Modeling the Activity

✹ Begin the session by asking students to tell what they know about the topic of the book you'll read aloud to them. Using a transparency of page 41, write these items under the "K" column.

✹ Ask students what they want to learn about the topic. Record these items under the "W" column.

✹ Read a few sections of the book. As you do so, stop at the end of each page or section and record new information in the "Cornell" section of the transparency. As a closing activity, review with students the "K" and "W" sections to see if any portion of the "Cornell" section affirmed what they already knew or provided answers to questions about topics they wanted to learn about.

On Their Own

Provide students with copies of pages 41 and 42. This activity works well for textbook reading.

K-W-Cornell

Name_____ Date_____

Story/Book/Article Title _____

Author _____

Before you read, complete the "K" and "W" portions of this page. As you read, stop at the end of each page, section, or chapter of your book and record in the Cornell section any main ideas, facts, statistics, examples, or quotations that you find interesting and informative. Take special note of any information that confirms the ideas you listed under the "K" column or any information that answers questions you wrote under your "W" column. Use the back of this page for additional items.

K (Tell what you KNOW already about this topic.)	W (Tell what you WANT to learn about this topic.)

CORNELL (Main idea, facts, and examples)   **Page Number(s)**

_____

_____

_____

_____

K-W-Cornell

Name_____ Date_____

Story/Book/Article Title _____

Author _____

Category	Excellent	Above Average	Average	Below Average
Quantity of WANT questions	5 questions	4 questions	3 questions	Less than 3 questions
Quality of WANT questions	Insightful	Interesting	Appropriate	Facts only
Quantity of Cornell entries	15 details	13 details	10 details	Less than 10
Quality of Cornell entries	Insightful	Interesting	Appropriate	Poor

Teacher's Comments: _____

_____

_____

_____

_____

_____

_____

_____

Theme Shape Poems

This activity is based on an idea developed by Dave Morice. In the November-December, 1999, newsletter of *Teachers & Writers,* Morice described how he developed "poemakers," which are special drawings that have blank lines for words. According to Morice, these poemakers are "springboards for writing." I ask my students to create their own central image for a book or story and write a poem in it. The poem should be about the book or story's theme.

Modeling the Activity

❉ Tell students you're going to create a Theme Shape Poem based on a story. Then display the sample image you created.

❉ Read aloud the story you've chosen for modeling the activity. Discuss the story's theme.

❉ Following the directions on the transparency of page 44, have students generate a list of descriptive words.

❉ As a class, decide on a central image. Then write a poem on the lines in the image, using the descriptive words students suggested and ideas based on the theme discussion.

On Their Own

Provide students with copies of pages 44 and 45 as well as the supplies (see Materials). It's also helpful to make sample Theme Shape Poems available to students.

Objective
Create a central literary image for an original poem

Materials

For the teacher:

❉ Transparency of page 44

❉ Sample image on a transparency (created by you)

❉ Blank transparency

For the student:

❉ Copies of pages 44 and 45

❉ Paper

❉ Markers

❉ Colored pencils

Stories for Modeling

"Hamish Mactavish is Eating a Bus" by Gordon Korman from *From One Experience to Another* (Tom Doherty Associates, 1997)

"Fountain of Youth" by Marc Talbert from *Trapped! Cages of Mind and Body* (Simon & Schuster, 1998)

"Alligator Mystique" by Barbara Robinson from *But That's Another Story* (Walker and Company, 1996)

Theme Shape Poems

Name_____ Date_____

Story/Book Title _____

Author _____

1 Theme Shape Poems are free-verse poems that fit within an important image from a story. Selecting an image and creating a list of descriptive words are important first steps in the creation of a Theme Shape Poem.

Identify six images that are important in your story or book.

1._____ 4._____

2._____ 5._____

3._____ 6._____

2 Brainstorm and record in the space below as many words as possible to describe the character(s), setting, plot, mood, and main idea of your story. (Remember to think about any special words, phrases, or descriptions used in the story, and any important pieces of dialogue.)

_____

_____

_____

_____

3 What is the theme of the story?

_____

_____

4 Think carefully about each of your six images. Select an image for your poem and draw a simple sketch on another sheet of paper. Make sure you create lines within your image so you have spaces for your words. When you've completed your drawing, think carefully about your list of words and the theme of the story. Write a rough draft of your poem. After you are satisfied with your rough draft, check all words for spelling. Finally, create a larger drawing and poem on a separate sheet of paper.

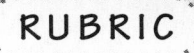

Theme Shape Poems

Name_____ Date_____

Story/Book Title _____

Author _____

Category	Excellent	Above Average	Average	Below Average
Central image	Insightful image	Significant image	Appropriate image	Unimportant image
Word choice	Vibrant word choice	Outstanding word choice	Good word choice	Very weak word choice
Spelling	All words correct	All words correct	One word misspelled	Several words misspelled
Appearance	Eye-catching	Attractive	Neat	Sloppy

Teacher's Comments: _____

_____

_____

_____

_____

_____

_____

_____

Is That a Fact?

Materials

For the teacher:

❀ Transparency of page 47

For the student:

❀ Copies of pages 47 and 48

Stories for Modeling

Shoes by Margery G. Nichelason (Carolrhoda Books, 1997)

On Your Feet! by Karin L. Badt (Children's Press, 1994)

Where Will This Shoe Take You? by Laurie Lawler (Walker and Co, 1996)

TEACHER TIP

When introducing this activity, pick a topic that's familiar to students yet still attention-getting.

Students often are not quite sure what constitutes a fact, a statistic, or an example. If we can give them a solid understanding of each, it will not only help students read nonfiction more effectively, but also improve their expository writing skills.

Modeling the Activity

❀ Use the transparency of page 47 to explain the definitions of a fact, a statistic, and an example.

❀ Tell students to listen carefully as you read aloud one of the books (see Stories for Modeling) or one of your own choosing. Pause at the end of each page or section and ask students if they heard any facts, statistics, or examples. Record the information they provide in the appropriate spaces on the transparency.

❀ In a follow-up session the next day, pass out copies of page 47 and continue to read aloud several more pages from the book. Again, pause after each page or section so students can record their facts, statistics, or examples. Pair students and have them share and verify the information they've recorded. Regroup as a class and have one person from each pair read the pair's most important fact, statistic, and example. Record the information in the appropriate place on the transparency.

On Their Own

Provide students with copies of page 47 and 48. Students may enjoy working in pairs on this activity.

Is That a Fact?

Name_____ Date_____

Story/Book/Article Title _____

Author _____

A FACT is something that can be verified or identified as being real.
   Example: The United States is part of the North American continent.

A STATISTIC is numerical information, or information explained using numbers.
   Example: Because of immigration, the population of the United States grew from
       23.2 million in 1850 to 76.2 million in 1900.

An EXAMPLE is specific information that can be used to represent a group as a whole.
   Example: The United States has fifty states, and Illinois is one of them.

Using your book, find and record facts, statistics, and examples in the proper spaces below.

Facts	Statistics	Examples
_____	_____	_____
_____	_____	_____
_____	_____	_____
_____	_____	_____
_____	_____	_____

Most Important Fact _____

_____

Most Important Statistic _____

_____

Most Important Example _____

_____

Is That a Fact?

Name_____   Date_____

Story/Book Title _____

Author _____

Category	Excellent	Above Average	Average	Below Average
Information in correct categories	All in correct categories	All in correct categories	Most in correct categories	Few in correct categories
Spelling	All items spelled correctly	All items spelled correctly	Some items misspelled	Several items misspelled
Quantity of items	Numerous	Several	Many	Some
Significance of information	Unique, little-known information	Most unknown pieces of information	Many unknown pieces of information	Mostly well-known information

Teacher's Comments: _____

_____

_____

_____

_____

_____

_____

_____

_____

25 Fun and Fabulous Literature Response Activities and Rubrics
Scholastic Professional Books

Pertinent Plot Parts

The plot of a story consists of those events that lead the story to its logical conclusion. This hands-on activity helps students make sense out of a story's plot and become aware of how a story's events fit together and "build" on one another.

Modeling the Activity

❋ Before reading aloud the story you've chosen for modeling this activity, tell students to pay close attention to the events in the story.

❋ After you've finished reading, ask students to identify important story events. Record these on the appropriate lines on the transparency of page 50. Read each of the items aloud and ask students to vote on each event's importance by raising one to five fingers—five indicating the most important.

❋ After the voting is completed, choose the six story events students felt were most important. Record them on the building block shapes on the transparency of page 51.

❋ Guide the modeling session discussion through steps 1, 2, and 3 on the Partner Portion list on page 51. (Note: An alternative is to provide students with the building block student page and allow them to work with partners as you move about the room listening, questioning, and encouraging pairs of students.) Students can complete step 4 on their own.

On Their Own

Provide students with copies of pages 50–52.

Objective
Evaluate plot events

Materials
For the teacher:
❋ Transparencies of pages 50 and 51

For the student:
❋ Copies of pages 50–52
❋ Scissors

Stories for Modeling
"Battleground" by Stephen King from *Read If You Dare* (Millbrook Press, 1997)

"A One-Woman Crime Wave" by Richard Peck from *A Long Way From Chicago* (Dial, 1998)

Pertinent Plot Parts

Name_____   Date_____

Story/Book Title _____

Author _____

The plot of a story consists of those events that lead the story to its logical conclusion.

Identify and list the 10 most important events in your story. Once you've finished your list, think carefully and rate each event on the scale next to it.

Important Events From My Story	Rating Scale

	Very Important			Not Important

① _____   5   4   3   2   1

② _____   5   4   3   2   1

③ _____   5   4   3   2   1

④ _____   5   4   3   2   1

⑤ _____   5   4   3   2   1

⑥ _____   5   4   3   2   1

⑦ _____   5   4   3   2   1

⑧ _____   5   4   3   2   1

⑨ _____   5   4   3   2   1

⑩ _____   5   4   3   2   1

25 Fun and Fabulous Literature Response Activities and Rubrics
Scholastic Professional Books

Pertinent Plot Parts

Name_____ Date_____

Record the six plot events you feel are most important in each of the shapes below. Cut out the shapes. Remove and save the Partner Portion at the bottom of the page.

Partner Portion

1. Arrange your Plot Parts in order as you explain your story to your partner.

2. Remove a Plot Part of your choosing and explain how the missing event changes the story.

3. Replace the Plot Part you removed. Now rearrange at least two Plot Parts and explain how this new sequence of story events changes the story.

4. Let your partner complete steps 1–3.

Pertinent Plot Parts

Name_____ Date_____

Story/Book Title _____

Author _____

Category	Excellent	Above Average	Average	Below Average
Completeness of rough draft list	All items completed	All items completed	One item missing	More than one item missing
Knowledge of story events	Substantial; identified major events	Familiar with most major events	Limited understanding of events	Little understanding of story events
Working with partner	Listened well; took turns and asked questions	Listened well; took turns	Adequate participation	Off task; uncooperative
Effort/ attitude	Enthusiastic	Appropriate	Adequate	Apathetic

Teacher's Comments: _____

_____

_____

_____

_____

_____

_____

Point of View

Point of View

Name _Javiel_   Date _October 12, 2002_

Story/Book Title _Fair Weather_

Author _Richard Peck_

The following questions will help you to determine what point of view an author is using to tell a story.

QUESTION 1: Does one of the characters tell the story and speak directly to you using the pronoun "I"?

Example: I was alone at night in my bed when suddenly I heard a loud noise. I jumped out of bed and ran to the window. My heart was pounding so hard, I could hear it in my ears.

Answer: If the author uses the pronoun "I" in this way, she or he is using the first-person point of view.

QUESTION 2: Do you "see" the story through one particular character's eyes and emotions, but this character doesn't talk directly to you using the pronoun "I"?

Example: Sam was alone in bed one night when he suddenly heard a loud noise outside his window. He sprang out of bed and ran to the window. His heart pounded so loudly that he could hear the thumping in his ears.

Answer: If the author tells his or her story through one character's eyes and emotions but doesn't have the character talk directly to the reader using the pronoun "I," then the author is using the limited third-person point of view.

Answer the questions below. Then use the back of this page to rewrite the introductory page of your book or story from a different point of view.

This story/book is written in _first-person_
(Identify either first-person or limited third-person point of view)

I know this book is written in this point of view because _the author uses "I." The story is told by Rosie Beckett who is fourteen years old._

25 Fun and Fabulous Literature Response Activities and Rubrics
Scholastic Professional Books   **55**

Objective

Compare and contrast literary points of view

Materials

For the teacher:

✺ Transparency of page 55

✺ Transparency of first paragraph of the story you choose to model the activity

For the student:

✺ Copies of pages 55 and 56

Stories for Modeling

First-Person

"Duel Identities" by David Lubar from *Lost & Found* (Tom Doherty, 2000)

Dovey Coe, A Novel by Frances O'Roark Dowell (Atheneum, 2000)

Limited Third-Person

"On the Bridge" by Todd Strasser from *Visions* (Bantam, 1987)

"A Wolf at the Door" by Tanith Lee from *A Wolf at the Door* (Simon & Schuster, 2000)

T his activity helps students recognize the point of view in the stories they read. It focuses on the two most common perspectives: first-person and limited third-person. Understanding point of view will also help students to use a consistent point of view in the stories they write.

Modeling the Activity

✷ One of the best ways to help students recognize how authors use different points of view is to read the first page of several novels. Students quickly learn to recognize the first-person point of view because the author uses the pronoun "I." At the same time, students quickly learn to recognize when the author tells his or her story through the eyes and emotions of a main character who doesn't directly address the reader using "I."

✷ After sharing several examples of points of view, the next step is to help students transfer this knowledge to their own writing. Students can do this by rewriting the first paragraph or the first page of a story or novel. Share with students this paragraph from *Dovey Coe, A Novel*, written in first-person.

My name is Dovey Coe, and I reckon it don't matter if you like me or not. I'm here to lay the record straight, to let you know them folks saying I done a terrible thing are liars. I aim to prove it, too. I hated Parnell Caraway as much as the next person, but I didn't kill him.

✹ Then share the same paragraph rewritten using the limited third-person point of view.

Twelve-year-old Dovey Coe didn't care whether people liked her or not. She didn't care about the terrible things people were saying about her. She didn't care that people thought she had killed Parnell Caraway. She knew they were wrong. Dead wrong—just like Parnell himself.

✹ Have students compare and contrast the two versions and tell which they think is more attention-grabbing.

✹ Share the story you chose to model the activity. After you've finished reading it aloud, display a copy of the first paragraph on an overhead transparency.

✹ Have students rewrite it using a different point of view. When students are done writing, have those who wish to share, do so. Once again, have students compare and contrast the different versions and decide which one is more attention-grabbing.

On Their Own

Provide students with copies of pages 55 and 56. Students can follow the directions on page 55 to complete this activity.

Point of View

Name _____ Date _____

Story/Book Title _____

Author _____

The following questions will help you determine what point of view an author is using to tell a story.

QUESTION 1: Does one of the characters tell the story and speak directly to you using the pronoun "I"?

Example: I was alone at night in my bed when suddenly I heard a loud noise. I jumped out of bed and ran to the window. My heart was pounding so hard, I could hear it in my ears.

Answer: If the author uses the pronoun "I" in this way, she or he is using the first-person point of view.

QUESTION 2: Do you "see" the story through one particular character's eyes and emotions, but this character doesn't talk directly to you using the pronoun "I"?

Example: Sam was alone in bed one night when he suddenly heard a loud noise outside his window. He sprang out of bed and ran to the window. His heart pounded so loudly that he could hear the thumping in his ears.

Answer: If the author tells his or her story through one character's eyes and emotions but doesn't have the character talk directly to the reader using the pronoun "I," then the author is using the limited third-person point of view.

Answer the questions below. Then use the back of this page to rewrite the introductory page of your book or story from a different point of view.

This story/book is written in _____

    (Identify either first-person or limited third-person point of view.)

I know this book is written in this point of view because _____

_____

_____

_____

Point of View

Name_____ Date_____

Story/Book Title _____

Author _____

Category	Excellent	Above Average	Average	Below Average
Point of view correctly identified in original story	Yes	Yes	Yes	No
Explanation of point of view indicates understanding	Thorough explanation	Complete explanation	Adequate explanation	Lacks understanding
Rewrite uses consistent point of view	Completely consistent	Almost completely consistent	A few errors in consistency	Several errors in consistency
Rewrite of first page complete	Complete in all details	Complete in almost all details	Complete in all details except a few	Incomplete

Teacher's Comments: _____

_____

_____

_____

_____

_____

Reading Review

This reading review activity is a fun, quick way to help students review all types of reading material.

Modeling the Activity

❋ Provide each student with a copy of page 58, which is a review chart for "Snow White and the Seven Dwarfs."

❋ Tell students they have 3 minutes to find a student who knows the answers to one or two items on the chart.

❋ Each student is allowed to put his or her initials on only two squares of another student's chart and may sign the same square only twice. (Sometimes I have students tape the charts to their backs!)

❋ When time is up, students come together as a group. Ask students who have initials in square one to raise their hands. These students then call on the person who has initialed his or her paper. That student gives the answer. To continue, you (or a student) move on to the next question. (Students learn very quickly not to initial a square if they don't know the answer because they realize they will be called on to supply the answer!)

❋ Read the material you've decided to use as a model. Together as a class, write questions in the boxes on the transparency of page 59.

On Their Own

Provide students with copies of pages 59 and 60. After students have completed page 59, create a class master review chart. Provide students with a copy of the class chart to use for the answering/initialing part of this activity.

Objective

Review fiction and nonfiction text

Materials

For the teacher:

❋ Transparency of page 59
❋ Tape (optional)

For the student:

❋ Copies of pages 58–60
❋ Copy of class master review chart

Stories for Modeling

Any 2–3 page magazine article or biography

Any chapter from a science or social studies textbook

> **TEACHER TIP**
>
> *I've found that this activity works best if I have a small group of students demonstrate it to the rest of the class.*

Reading Review

Reading Review chart for "Snow White and the Seven Dwarfs." Find a person who can…

Tell what put Snow White into a deep sleep.	Tell how Snow White escaped her execution in the woods.	Name all seven dwarfs.
Tell the occupation of the dwarfs.	Tell the reason Snow White was marked for death.	Tell how the stepmother's disguise represented her true nature.
Hum any part of a song from the movie version of Snow White.	Tell how Snow White awoke from her sleep.	Compare and contrast Snow White with Cinderella.

Reading Review

Name_____ Date_____

Story/Book/Article Title _____

Author _____

Write a review statement in each square below. Be sure to use active words to begin each review item. Some active words are: name, explain, compare, contrast, describe, tell, define, summarize, create, predict, conclude, organize, and evaluate.

Reading Review

Name_____ Date_____

Story/Book Title _____

Author _____

Category	Excellent	Above Average	Average	Below Average
Quantity of items	Completed all assigned	Completed all assigned	Completed most assigned	Many left incomplete
Clarity of review items	Clearly focused; completely understandable	Clear meaning throughout	At times a bit confusing	Unclear in many instances
Use of active words	Used active words with all items	Used active words with almost all items	Used active words with many items	Few active words used
Significance of review items	All related to important ideas from material	Almost all related to important ideas	Many related to important ideas	Few related to important ideas

Teacher's Comments: _____

_____

_____

_____

_____

_____

_____

25 Fun and Fabulous Literature Response Activities and Rubrics
Scholastic Professional Books

It Happened in a Flash (Back)!

It Happened in a Flash (Back)!

Name _Josie_ Date _2/9/02_
Story/Book Title _My Side of the Mountain_
Author _Jean Craighead George_

Authors use a technique called a "flashback" to give readers information that happened before the story's opening scene. Often the author will have the main character recall an episode or even experience a dream to give the reader the necessary information. As the story continues, the past and present events are woven together and brought to a satisfactory conclusion.

Complete the chart below. When you are done, fold the paper along the dotted lines so the arrows match up. This will show you how the story's present and past are brought together.

As the story opens, these are the things happening in the present. (Be sure to identify characters, place, and time.)	In the flashback, I learn the following information	The past and present events come together in the end. (Tell how past events relate to present ones.)
The book begins with Sam's journal description of a terrible snow storm.	Sam left for the woods in the spring because he wanted to live indepen-dently in the woods.	Sam has learned about how to survive and planned well. He survived the terrible storm.

Flashback is a literary device that authors use to give readers information that happened prior to the story's opening scene. The author may have a character recall an episode ("I remember the time when…") or experience a dream such as the one Ebenezer Scrooge experiences with the Ghost of Christmas Past in *A Christmas Carol*.

This activity will help students recognize a flashback and demonstrate how it is used as a connecting device to bridge a story's past with its present.

Modeling the Activity

❋ Begin by first explaining what flashbacks are and how and why authors use the device in stories. Ask students to tell about television shows or movies they've seen that contain flashbacks.

❋ Read the story you've chosen for modeling the activity.

❋ Distribute copies of page 62 and let students work with a partner to complete the chart. When the entire group reassembles, have three different partner pairs tell the information that should be listed under each category as you record it on the transparency of page 62.

On Their Own

This activity will only work with books that include flashback. Provide students with copies of pages 62 and 63.

Objective
Explain and describe the use of flashback

Materials
For the teacher:
❋ Transparency of page 62
For the student:
❋ Copies of pages 62 and 63

Stories for Modeling
Help! I'm Trapped in the First Day of School by Todd Strasser (Scholastic, 1994)

Crash by Jerry Spinnelli (Knopf, 1996)

It Happened in a Flash (Back)!

Name_____ Date_____

Story/Book Title _____

Author _____

Authors use a technique called a "flashback" to give readers information that happened before the story's opening scene. Often the author will have the main character recall an episode or even experience a dream to give the reader the necessary information. As the story continues, the past and present events are woven together and brought to a satisfactory conclusion.

Complete the chart below. When you are done, fold the paper along the dotted lines so the arrows match up. This will show you how the story's present and past are brought together.

As the story opens, these are the things happening in the present. (Be sure to identify characters, place, and time.)	In the flashback, I learn the following information.	The past and present events come together in the end. (Tell how past events relate to present ones.)

25 Fun and Fabulous Literature Response Activities and Rubrics
Scholastic Professional Books

It Happened in a Flash (Back)!

Name_____ Date_____

Story/Book Title _____

Author _____

Category	Excellent	Above Average	Average	Below Average
Knowledge of story events	Substantial	Familiar	Limited	Little understanding
Coherency of listed items	All listed items related to story as a whole	All listed items related to story as a whole	Many items related to story as a whole	Few items related to story as a whole
Quantity of listed items	6 or more items	5 items	4 items	3 items or less
Clarity of meaning	Clearly focused; completely understandable	Clear meaning throughout	At times a bit confusing	Confusing in many places

Teacher's Comments: _____

_____

_____

_____

_____

_____

_____

_____

Mini Mind-Map Scrapbook

Stories for Modeling

"Hands in the Darkness" by Peter D. Sieruta from *Help Wanted: Short Stories About Young People Working* (Little, Brown, 1997)

"What the Princess Discarded" by Barbara Ann Porte from *Birthday Surprises: Ten Great Stories to Unwrap* (Beech Tree, 1995)

"Mind Mapping" can be an especially useful tool for students who favor a more visual learning approach, have difficulty creating linear outlines, or have trouble taking notes. In one respect, Mind Mapping is a sophisticated form of webbing, a learning tool with which many students are already familiar.

This Mini Mind-Maps activity combines some of the elements of Mind Mapping with scrapbooking, resulting in a fun, creative activity.

Modeling the Activity

✳ To introduce this activity, have students tell the story of "The Three Little Pigs." While they relate the story, draw the face of a wolf in the middle of a transparency. On "paths" branching from the wolf, sketch the houses of each of the pigs. In an arc above the three houses, write, "Not by the hair of my chinny chin chin. We will not let you in." Underneath the face of the wolf, write, "Then I'll huff and I'll puff, and I'll blow your house in."

❈ Explain that the unifying element (or main element that relates to all three pigs) is the wolf, so its image is placed in the center of the page. The three houses are minor story elements, so they appear around the wolf. Finally, the two quotations are essential information that add to the understanding of the story.

❈ Ask students to suggest ways this Mind-Map image could be transferred and transformed as a scrapbook page. One suggestion might be to use images of houses students have drawn or cut out from magazines. They might also add borders. (It may be helpful to have various samples of scrapbook supplies in your room so students can see what kinds of materials are available.)

❈ Finally, read the story you've chosen to use for modeling the activity. As a group, complete the trans-parency of page 66. Then have students draw a sketch of a proposed scrapbook page.

On Their Own

Provide students with copies of pages 66 and 67. Tell them to be prepared to submit page 66 along with their final Mini Mind-Map Scrapbook to you.

TEACHER TIP
This is an especially good book-sharing strategy. It serves as a visual "booktalk" and helps sell the book to other students.

Mini Mind-Map Scrapbook

Name_____ Date_____

Story/Book Title _____

Author _____

Complete this planning page to help you outline your Mini Mind Map.

Identify two possible unifying elements: _____ and _____

Identify four possible minor elements. As you do, explain the visual representation (picture or symbol) you could use to represent the element and identify examples and/or quotations that support and explain each of the minor elements. Be sure to include the page number of where you found your support.

Minor Element_____

   Possible Visual_____

   Quotation/Example _____ Page_____

Minor Element_____

   Possible Visual_____

   Quotation/Example _____ Page_____

Minor Element_____

   Possible Visual_____

   Quotation/Example _____ Page_____

Minor Element_____

   Possible Visual_____

   Quotation/Example _____ Page_____

Use the back of this page to draw a sketch of your Mini Mind-Map Scrapbook.

25 Fun and Fabulous Literature Response Activities and Rubrics
Scholastic Professional Books

Mini Mind-Map Scrapbook

Name_____ Date_____

Story/Book Title _____

Author _____

Category	Excellent	Above Average	Average	Below Average
Unifying element	Insightful; imaginative	Creative image	Good image	Not story's central image
Minor elements	Insightful imaginative images; 3–4 images	Creative images; 3 images	Good images; 3 images	Not related; less than 3 images
Appearance	Eye-catching; excellent detail	Attractive; very good detail	Neat; some detail	Sloppy; incomplete
Examples/ quotations	Significant; best possible	Related to elements	Some are not related	Not related; insignificant

Teacher's Comments: _____

_____

_____

_____

_____

_____

_____

_____

The Answer Is...

"The Answer Is…" activity is an excellent way to review fiction and nonfiction books and an easy way for you to check reading comprehension. In this activity, one student supplies the answers, and that student's partner or group members supply the question(s) that correctly match the answers.

Modeling the Activity

✳ Read aloud the story you've chosen to use for modeling the activity. When the story is finished, tell students that you are going to supply an answer, and they will have to supply a question that correctly matches the answer. Here is an example for the story "Under the Wire."

> The Answer Is…A bag full of oranges, apples, and candy.
> The Question Is…What did the conductor gently drop from the train for Roberto and his sister?

✳ Write the answers in the squares of the transparency of page 69. As students supply questions, write them on the transparency also.

On Their Own

Provide students with copies of pages 69 and 70.

If students decide to work with a partner, each student must read the same book. (Here is an opportunity for struggling readers to "buddy read" the same book with another student.) After the pair is done reading, one student writes answers for the first half of the book, and the other student writes answers for the second half of the book. Student pairs then take turns providing the questions.

Students who work in a larger group also read the same book. When they are done reading, members divide up the book and write answers and questions for their assigned pages. Within the group, members take turns with their answers and refer to the book for clarification.

Objective
Review fiction and nonfiction text

Materials
For the teacher:
❀ Transparency of page 69

For the student:
❀ Copies of pages 69 and 70

Stories for Modeling
"Under the Wire" by Francisco Jimenez from *The Circuit: Stories from the Life of a Migrant Child* (Scholastic, 1997)

"Testing" by Tamora Pierce from *Lost and Found* (Tom Doherty Associates, 2000)

The Answer Is...

Name_____ Date_____

Story/Book Title_____ Author_____

The Answer Is...	The Answer Is...	The Answer Is...
The Question Is...	The Question Is...	The Question Is...
The Answer Is...	The Answer Is...	The Answer Is...
The Question Is...	The Question Is...	The Question Is...
The Answer Is...	The Answer Is...	The Answer Is...
The Question Is...	The Question Is...	The Question Is...

The Answer Is...

Name_____   Date_____

Story/Book Title _____

Author _____

Category	Excellent	Above Average	Average	Below Average
Quantity of answers	Completed all assigned	Completed all assigned	Completed most assigned	Most incomplete
Clarity of answers and questions	Clearly focused; completely understandable	Clear meaning throughout	Some unclear	Unclear; confusing in many areas
Significance of answers and questions	All related to important ideas from the book	Almost all related to important ideas	Most related to important ideas	Few related to important ideas
Accuracy of answers and questions	All matched	All matched	Most matched	Few matched

Teacher's Comments: _____

_____

_____

_____

_____

_____

_____

 25 Fun and Fabulous Literature Response Activities and Rubrics
Scholastic Professional Books

Thirty-Second Vocabulary

Objective
Increase vocabulary

Materials
For the teacher:
❋ Transparency of page 73
❋ Sticky-notes
❋ Thesaurus
For the student:
❋ Copies of pages 73–75
❋ Blank transparency
❋ Thesaurus
❋ Art supplies

Stories for Modeling
"Hacker" by Sinclair Smith from *Thirteen Tales of Horrors* (Scholastic, 1991)

Mary on Horseback by Rosemary Wells (Dial, 1998)

"As True As She Wants It" by David Skinner from *Thundershine: Tales of Metakids* (Simon & Schuster, 1999)

Getting students to improve and increase their vocabulary (whether it's for reading, writing, or speaking) is every teacher's goal. After all, almost every book a student encounters in a school setting has new words that can be learned.

The Thirty-Second Vocabulary activity will help students increase and retain new vocabulary words from the books they read. This hands-on, no-holds-barred activity is entertaining, enlightening, and educational.

Modeling the Activity

❋ As you read aloud the story you've chosen for modeling the activity, use sticky-notes to indicate one or two pages that contain words you wish to go back to at the end of the story. After finishing the story, explain to students that the tagged pages contain words that you would like them to know well enough that they become a part of their reading and writing vocabularies.

✺ Read the sentences containing the words. Record them on the synonym strip portion of the transparency of page 73.

✺ Have one group of students supply synonyms for the vocabulary words using only context clues, while another group of students uses a thesaurus to supply synonyms. Record synonyms for each of the vocabulary words on the transparency. Have students read each sentence aloud, inserting a synonym directly after they say the vocabulary word. This repeated reading helps students link the new vocabulary word with a synonym they already know.

✺ The second portion of this modeling session is to "teach" one of the new vocabulary words by using or explaining the word in a song, poem, skit, game, or riddle, or by using any of the 35 other ways listed on page 74. (You may want to post a copy of the list on a bulletin board.)

✺ Model a few ways to teach a word within a 30-second time frame. The more examples students see, the more likely they will be to use a variety of activities when they share their own vocabulary words.

On Their Own

Provide students with copies of pages 73 and 75. Also have on hand supplies they might need for the projects listed on page 74.

Thirty-Second Vocabulary

Name_____ Date_____

Story/Book Title _____

Author _____

Follow the steps below to complete this activity.

As you read your book, be on the lookout for unfamiliar words that you'd like to learn. When you come across one, put a sticky-note on that page so you can return to the word after you've finished reading. Remember: Being on the lookout for new words shouldn't interfere with your reading enjoyment—so don't tag every word or every page!

   After you've finished your story or book, go through your tagged pages and select three words. In the spaces below, copy the sentence that each word appears in and write three synonyms for each of your words. (The synonyms should be words you know.)

SYNONYM STRIP 1   Word:_____

Sentence: _____

_____

Three synonyms: _____ _____ _____

SYNONYM STRIP 2   Word: _____

Sentence:_____

_____

Three synonyms: _____ _____ _____

SYNONYM STRIP 3 Word:_____

Sentence:_____

_____

Three synonyms: _____ _____ _____

Thirty-Second Vocabulary

Name_____ Date_____

You have 30 seconds to teach each of your words to your classmates. You may use the following methods or another one with the approval of your teacher:

song	poem	skit	musical piece
dance	illustration	joke	riddle
game	video	demonstration	pantomime
object	costume	diagram	poster
advertisement	banner	cartoon	chart
debate	display	film strip	graph
list	mobile	newscast	painting
photograph	puppet show	rap	scrapbook
experiment	sculpture	sports analysis	story
symbols	time line	picture dictionary	encyclopedia entry

25 Fun and Fabulous Literature Response Activities and Rubrics
Scholastic Professional Books

Thirty-Second Vocabulary

Name_____   Date_____

Story/Book Title _____

Author _____

Category	Excellent	Above Average	Average	Below Average
Completion of student page	All items completed	All items completed	One item missing	Several items missing
Effort/ Attitude	Enthusiastic	Appropriate	Adequate	Apathetic
Synonyms	Excellent examples	Very good examples	Good examples	Poor examples
Performance	Extremely well-organized; effective	Very well organized; effective	Good organization; adequate	Unorganized; ineffective

Teacher's Comments: _____

_____

_____

_____

_____

_____

_____

_____

Person-Pouch Performance

Objective
Create artifacts and present a monologue based on a biographical or autobiographical text

Materials

For the teacher:
✿ Transparency of pages 78 and 79
✿ Note cards
✿ Biography or autobiography
✿ Chosen artifacts
✿ Pouch or bag

For the student:
✿ Copies of pages 78–80
✿ Chosen artifacts
✿ Note cards
✿ Pouch or bag

Stories for Modeling

Nellie Bly: Daredevil Reporter by Charles Fredeen (Lerner Publications, 2000)

Prisoner for Peace: Ang San Suu Kyi and Burma's Struggle for Democracy by John Parenteau (Morgan Reynolds, Inc., 1994)

John Paul Jones: Father of the U.S. Navy by Norma Jean Lutz (Chelsea House, 2000)

Howard Gardner's Theory of Multiple Intelligences, which he describes in his book *Frames of Mind: The Theory of Multiple Intelligences* (Basic Books, 1983), supports the idea that people are "smart" in different ways. (The saying that is shared at many teacher workshops is: Don't ask how smart you are but rather ask how are you smart.) Gardner believes there are many intelligences. So far, he has identified the following: linguistic, logical/mathematical, naturalist, spatial, bodily/kinesthetic, musical, interpersonal, and intrapersonal. The Person-Pouch Performance activity attempts to tap into as many intelligences as possible, but it especially fosters the linguistic, interpersonal, and spatial intelligences.

Modeling the Activity

✺ This is the only activity I've included in this book in which you don't read the book prior to modeling the activity for students. It is much more dramatic to walk into the classroom carrying your Person Pouch filled with artifacts and proceed to address the class as Nellie Bly than it is to read portions of the book and then try to present a first-person performance.

✹ Because it takes a lot of time to prepare a Person-Pouch Performance, choose a person about whom you'd like to know more. (Also, try to choose a person with whom students are not familiar and who is not already a part of the curriculum.) Follow the steps on page 78.

✹ After your performance, use the transparencies of pages 78 and 79 and explain exactly what you did to prepare for the day's performance. This "Think Aloud" will help students have a better idea of what they will need to do in order to prepare their own Person-Pouch Performance.

On Their Own

Provide students with copies of pages 78–80. This is a long-term activity. Allow adequate time for students to read their books and prepare for their performances.

TEACHER TIP

The Person-Pouch Performance activity can be used with fictional books as well. Students "become" the main character in their books and tell the events of the story from the character's point of view.

Person-Pouch Performance

Name_____ Date_____

Story/Book Title _____

Author _____

A Person-Pouch Performance is a 5–10 minute first-person presentation in which you assume the identity of the person you read about. During the presentation, you show artifacts or objects that relate in a special way to your person. To prepare your Person-Pouch Performance, follow the steps below and complete the planning information on the next page.

1. Read an interesting biography or autobiography of the person you've chosen. To help you keep track of special events, names, and important facts, create a time line on a series of note cards (or a piece of paper) by stopping at the end of each chapter to record your information.

2. After you've finished reading your book, go through your note cards and decide on the important details that you'd like to share with your audience. Remember: You will be talking to the audience in the first-person as if the audience has gathered as a group in a living room to hear this person speak about his or her life.

3. Create or find artifacts that you can use during your performance to explain your person's life. For example, if you are portraying Abraham Lincoln, you might make a stovepipe hat out of black construction paper. You should plan to have at least five artifacts to use during your performance.

4. Plan what you are going to say by going through your note cards. It's important that you relate only the important events and details of your person's life and concentrate on his or her most important accomplishments.

5. Rehearse your presentation several times. Practice in front of a mirror so you can see yourself. Ask a friend or a parent to watch your performance to be sure you are speaking loudly and clearly enough, and to be sure all the information in your presentation is organized correctly.

6. Put your artifacts into a bag, pouch, backpack, or box and take it to class on the day you are scheduled to do your performance. Relax and have fun giving your presentation!

   (Remember to get approval from your parents and teacher for the artifacts you plan to bring to school.)

25 Fun and Fabulous Literature Response Activities and Rubrics
Scholastic Professional Books

Person-Pouch Performance
(continued)

Name_____ Date_____

Answering the questions below will help you prepare for your Person-Pouch Performance.

(1) During what time period did this person live?

(2) In what country or region of the country did this person live?

(3) How will the time period, country, and region where this person lived affect my performance? Will I use any special words or terms? Will I use an accent?

_____

(4) When I'm pretending to be this person during my performance, how old will I pretend to be? How will I let the audience know my age? _____

_____

(5) What special events will I include in my performance? (Some possible topics to include: date and place of birth, family members, education, travel, special obstacles or setbacks, achievements, historical events that affected this person's life, any special sayings for which this person is noted, date and place of death.) Remember: Your performance should not be a listing of events. You should let your audience know the feelings of this person as well.

_____

_____

_____

(6) What possible artifacts or objects can I use during my performance that will let the audience know more about this person? (You should include at least five objects.)

_____

_____

_____

My rehearsal schedule is below:

By myself _____   For a friend _____   For a parent or other adult _____

Person-Pouch Performance

Name_____ Date_____

Story/Book Title _____

Author _____

Category	Excellent	Above Average	Average	Below Average
Presentation	Exceptional	Well-prepared	Needed more rehearsal	Not prepared
Organization of information	Clearly focused; excellent choice of details	Clearly focused; very good choice of details	Confusing in a few parts; good details	Unorganized; few details
Use of significanct artifacts	5 objects; each well-chosen	4 objects; each important	3 objects; each good	Less than 3 objects; not significant
Use of student planning sheet	Thorough use	Significant use	Adequate	Little use

Teacher's Comments: _____

_____

_____

_____

_____

_____

_____

_____

Succinct Sentences

> **Nightjohn** by Gary Paulsen
>
> 1. Sarny, the twelve-year old slave of Clel Waller, acts dumb but actually learns a lot – especially about the man named Night John.
> 2. Sarny, while working under the mistress's window, over hears a conversation about Night John, who is bought for $1,000.
> 3. Sarny meets John, who teaches her the letter A in trade for a lip of tobacco.
> 4. Night John, after teaching Sarny B and C, tells her that he escaped north but returned to teach slaves to read.
> 5. Sarny writes the word "BAG" in the dirt, and when Clel discovers her, he whips Mammy and cuts off John's two toes.
> 6. Night John runs away, creates a school, and returns to teach Sarny and a few other slaves to read and write.
>
> Caleb

T he Succinct Sentences activity demands that students be active listeners and meaning-makers. Students must carefully listen to each chapter as it's read aloud and then create a one-sentence summary. At the completion of the book, students will have a complete overview of the book written in a few succinct sentences.

Modeling the Activity

☀ Demonstrate what a summary sentence is by asking students to create a summary sentence of "The Three Little Pigs." (An example might be: "The Three Little Pigs" is a story about a wolf who tries to catch and eat the little pigs by destroying their houses but who is himself eaten in the end.) Write suggested sentences on an overhead transparency and edit until the class is satisfied with its sentence. (This step will help you model editing techniques.)

Objective
Listen actively and compose succinct summary sentences

Materials
For the teacher:
✿ Blank transparency
✿ Transparency of page 83
✿ Tape recorder (optional)
For each student:
✿ Copies of pages 83 and 84

Stories for Modeling
Number the Stars by Lois Lowry (Houghton, 1989)

Call It Courage by Armstrong Sperry (Macmillan, 1940)

Nightjohn by Gary Paulsen (Delacorte Press, 1993)

✹ Explain that each day you will read a chapter from the selected book and require students to write a one-sentence summary after that day's reading. Tell students to keep their sentences together on one page and leave several lines between each sentence for rewriting and editing. (Note: You may want to tape-record your oral reading so students who are absent can listen to the tape when they return to class.)

✹ After each day's reading and writing, introduce a rewriting and/or editing strategy. The strategies you choose will depend upon the needs of your students. For example, you might wish to emphasize some of the following:

- writing in the active voice;
- placing prepositional phrases correctly;
- using verb tenses consistently;
- using descriptive, precise words;
- punctuating all sentences correctly.

On Their Own

Provide students with copies of pages 83 and 84. I ask students to put the final draft of their sentences on another sheet of paper. I also tell them to be prepared to turn in page 83 for review and/or assessment.

TEACHER TIP

Have fun writing one-sentence summaries of other familiar fairy tales. Students enjoy seeing how succinct their sentences can get!

Succinct Sentences

Name_____   Date _____

Story/Book Title_____   Author _____

Summarize each chapter in the book you are reading by writing one succinct sentence. You can use this page for writing, rewriting, and editing your sentences. Don't erase! Instead, cross out words and add others. These corrections will show your teacher what you have done to improve your work. Finally, write your revised succinct sentences on the lines labeled SS. If your book has more than five chapters, use the back of this page to continue your work.

Chapter 1_____

_____

SS _____

Chapter 2 _____

_____

SS_____

Chapter 3 _____

_____

SS _____

Chapter 4_____

_____

SS _____

Chapter 5_____

_____

SS _____

Succinct Sentences

Name_____ Date_____

Story/Book Title _____

Author_____ Number of Chapters_____

Category	Excellent	Above Average	Average	Below Average
Clarity of sentences	Clearly focused; completely understandable	Clear meaning throughout	At times a bit confusing	Incoherent in many places
Editing and revising	Skillful use of editing and revising	Significant editing and revising	Some use of editing and revising	Few instances of editing and revising
Accuracy of chapter main ideas	Each chapter's sentence is insightful	Each chapter's sentence states main idea	Most sentences state main idea	Few sentences state main idea
Mechanics (grammar, punctuation, spelling, and capitalization)	Skillful use of mechanics	Very few errors in mechanics	A few errors in mechanics	Several errors in mechanics

Teacher's Comments: _____

_____

_____

_____

_____

_____

25 Fun and Fabulous Literature Response Activities and Rubrics
Scholastic Professional Books

Personal Perspective

Personal Perspective

Name Rebecca   Date December 15
Story/Book Title The View from Saturday
Author E. L. Konigsburg

Different characters can be involved in exactly the same events and have two entirely different perspectives. Think of two people riding together in the front car of an enormous roller coaster. One person loves roller coasters and has a wonderful time. The other person is horrified and becomes ill with fright from the experience. Same seat. Same roller coaster. But the two people will tell their friends very different stories about their experience because each had a very different perspective.

The book you've read tells a story told from the different perspectives of various characters. Explain these characters' perspectives by answering the questions below.

The common event that the characters share is Preparing for and participating in an Academic Bowl.

In the space below, identify each character and explain HOW the event affected that character and WHY the event affected that character the way it did.

Character's Name Julian

HOW: Julian had to work hard to get the other students to accept him.

WHY: Since Julian is different from the other students, they don't accept him right away.

A story told through the eyes of two or more characters can be very intriguing. This type of story allows students to see how people can be affected very differently by the same set of events. The Personal Perspective activity encourages students to recognize various perspectives and analyze why characters react the way they do to circumstances.

Objective
Compare and contrast various characters' perspectives

Materials

For the teacher:

❀ Transparencies of pages 86 and 87

❀ Copies of *Joyful Noise: Poems for Two Voices*

For each student:

❀ Copies of pages 86–88

Stories for Modeling

Flying Solo by Ralph Fletcher (Houghton Mifflin, 1998)

Bat 6 by Virginia Euwer Wolff (Scholastic, 1998)

Modeling the Activity

❁ One of the best ways to introduce students to what "perspective" means is to perform "Honeybees" from Paul Fleischman's delightful *Joyful Noise: Poems for Two Voices* (Harper, 1988). In this poem, two honeybees, one a worker and the other a queen, tell what it's really like to be a honeybee. Of course, they lead entirely different lives while living in the same hive.

❁ Ask students to provide other examples where two characters may view the same event "through different eyes." Record this list on the board.

❁ Once students have a general idea of what perspective means, read aloud portions of one of the suggested books (see Stories for Modeling) and have students compare and contrast the characters' different perspectives and record their ideas on the transparencies of pages 86 and 87.

On Their Own

Provide students with copies of pages 86–88.

Personal Perspective

Name_____ Date_____

Story/Book Title _____

Author_____

Different characters can be involved in exactly the same events and have two entirely different perspectives. Think of two people riding together in the front car of an enormous roller coaster. One person loves roller coasters and has a wonderful time. The other person is horrified and becomes ill with fright from the experience. Same seat. Same roller coaster. But the two people will tell their friends very different stories about their experiences because each had a very different perspective.

The book you've read tells a story told from the different perspectives of various characters. Explain these characters' perspectives by answering the questions below.

The common event that the characters share is _____

_____

_____.

In the space provided, identify each character and explain HOW the event affected that character and WHY the event affected that character the way it did.

Character's Name _____

HOW: _____   WHY: _____

_____   _____

_____   _____

_____   _____

_____   _____

_____   _____

25 Fun and Fabulous Literature Response Activities and Rubrics
Scholastic Professional Books

Personal Perspective

(continued)

Character's Name _____

HOW: _____   WHY: _____

_____   _____

_____   _____

_____   _____

_____   _____

_____   _____

Character's Name _____

HOW: _____   WHY: _____

_____   _____

_____   _____

_____   _____

_____   _____

_____   _____

Character's Name _____

HOW: _____   WHY: _____

_____   _____

_____   _____

_____   _____

_____   _____

Personal Perspective

Name_____   Date_____

Story/Book Title _____

Author _____

Category	Excellent	Above Average	Average	Below Average
Common event is described accurately and completely	Accurate; with complete details	Complete; accurate	In general terms only	Incomplete and/or inaccurate
HOW event is accurate with detail	Accurate; detailed	Accurate; complete	Mostly complete and accurate	Vague description; little detail
WHY event is accurate with detail	Accurate; detailed	Accurate; complete	Mostly complete and accurate	Vague description; little detail
Mechanics (Punctuation, spelling, grammar, and capitalization	Skillful use of mechanics	Very few errors in mechanics	A few errors in mechanics	Several errors in mechanics

Teacher's Comments: _____

_____

_____

_____

_____

_____

25 Fun and Fabulous Literature Response Activities and Rubrics
Scholastic Professional Books

Quality Questions

It's a common practice in many classrooms for the teacher to ask all the questions, and for students to provide the answers. With the Quality Questions activity, students not only answer the questions, but they create them as well. Asking good questions will help them review information and discover any topic areas they need to explore in more depth.

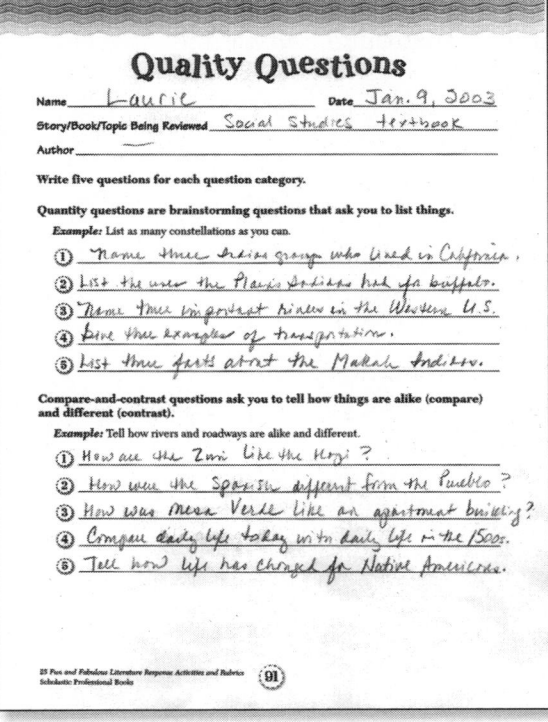

Objective
Review fiction and nonfiction text by asking five types of questions

Materials
For the teacher:
- Transparency with category listings (see page 91)
- Transparencies of pages 91 and 92

For each student:
- Copies of pages 91–93

Modeling the Activity

- The five question types I teach students to ask are quantity questions, compare-and-contrast questions, questions about feelings, opinion questions, and "what if" questions. Examples are provided on the next page and on student pages 91 and 92.

- To introduce students to the different types of questions, select a familiar topic. For example, you may want to pick a topic such as "Eating at McDonald's."

- To begin the session, list the different categories of questions on an overhead transparency and ask students to generate questions for each category. (See the example questions that follow for the "Eating at McDonald's" topic.)

QUANTITY QUESTIONS ask students to list things.

Example: What are the different types of sandwiches you can buy at McDonald's?

Stories for Modeling

Topic for Grades 4–6: Fossils

Stone Girl, Bone Girl by Laurence Anholt (Orchard, 1999)

Fossil Feud: The Rivalry of the First American Dinosaur Hunters by Thom Holmes (Messner, 1998)

Topic for Grades 6–8: Greek Mythology

Greek Myths and Legends by Anthony Masters (Peter Bedrick Books, 2000)

Greek Myths: Ulysses and the Trojan War by Anna Claybourne (EDC Publishing, 1999)

COMPARE AND CONTRAST QUESTIONS ask students to tell how two things are alike (compare) and how they are different (contrast).

> *Example:* How is the hamburger that you buy at McDonald's alike and different from the one you make at home?

> *Note:* Compare-and-contrast questions can also be forced association questions, such as: How are the drinking straws used at McDonald's alike and different from roadway tunnels?

FEELING QUESTIONS ask students to tell their personal feelings about a topic.

> *Example:* Which McDonald's give-away toy excited you the most and why?

> *Note:* Feeling questions can also involve personification. For example: How would a McDonald's trash can feel at closing time?

OPINION QUESTIONS ask students to give their opinions about a topic.

> *Example:* In your opinion, should McDonald's restaurants stay open all day and all night?

"WHAT IF" QUESTIONS ask students to open up their thinking and imagine "what if."

> *Example:* What would happen if McDonald's became so famous and overcrowded that children could only eat in the restaurants between 3:00 P.M. and 5:00 P.M. during the week and never on Sundays?

✺ Once you feel your students are familiar with the different types of questions, distribute copies of pages 91 and 92 and identify the book or story about which they are to write questions. (If students need more practice, choose a book, but continue helping students to generate the different types of questions.)

✺ As a final activity, gather and redistribute student pages, and invite student groups to discuss the answers to the questions.

On Their Own

Provide students with copies of pages 91–93. If pairs or groups of students have read the same book, have them exchange question sheets and answer one another's questions. Allow time to discuss answers.

Quality Questions

Name_____ Date_____

Story/Book/Topic Being Reviewed _____

Author _____

Write five questions for each question category.

Quantity questions are brainstorming questions that ask you to list things.

Example: List as many Greek heroes as you can.

1. _____

2. _____

3. _____

4. _____

5. _____

Compare-and-contrast questions ask you to tell how things are alike (compare) and different (contrast).

Example: Tell how rivers and roadways are alike and different.

1. _____

2. _____

3. _____

4. _____

5. _____

Quality Questions

Feeling questions ask you to tell what your personal feelings are about a topic.

Example: How would you feel if the main character in this book invited you to his or her birthday party?

1. _____

2. _____

3. _____

4. _____

5. _____

Opinion questions ask you to give your opinion about a topic.

Example: In your opinion, were the main character's decisions wise or unwise? Why?

1. _____

2. _____

3. _____

4. _____

5. _____

"What if" questions ask you to open your mind and imagine "What if..."

Example: What if this story had an entirely different setting?

1. _____

2. _____

3. _____

4. _____

5. _____

Quality Questions

Name_____ Date_____

Story/Book Title _____

Author _____

Category	Excellent	Above Average	Average	Below Average
Quantity of questions	Completed all assigned	Completed all assigned	Completed most assigned	Most left incomplete
Clarity of questions	Clearly focused; completely understandable	Clear meaning throughout	At times a bit confusing	Unclear in many instances
Significance of questions	All related to important ideas from the book	Almost all related to important ideas	Most related to important ideas	Few related to important ideas
Questions in categories	All questions fit correct categories	Almost all questions fit categories	Most of the questions fit categories	Few of the questions fit categories

Teacher's Comments: _____

_____

_____

_____

_____

_____

_____

Dialogue Play

Objective
Analyze dialogue

Materials

For the teacher:
✿ Dialogue play written on note cards (see page 95)
✿ Bowl and spoon
✿ Food mixture for play (optional)

For each student:
✿ Copy of page 96
✿ Scissors

Stories for Modeling

Yo! Yes? by Chris Raschka (Orchard Books, 1993)

Ring! Yo? by Chris Raschka (Dorling Kindersley, 2000)

That's Good! That's Bad! by Margery Cuyler (Henry Holt, 1991)

This activity helps students to comprehend the importance of dialogue in advancing a story line and in developing a character.

Modeling the Activity

✷ Explain to students that in the hands of a skillful author, dialogue usually follows some basic rules, such as:

- It advances the action of the story in some way;
- It is consistent with each character's personality;
- It is conversational.

✷ Dialogue also provides clues to a character's emotions. For instance, note how the different use of tag lines changes the meaning of the following dialogue:

"What do you want?" Jeff asked angrily. "Nothing," Tim coldly replied.

"What do you want?" Jeff sighed. "Nothing," Tim whispered.

✷ Before you read aloud the story you've chosen for modeling the activity, perform the Dialogue Play on the next page. (Suggestions: Take nine students into the hall and give each one a card with his or her line of dialogue. Rehearse quickly. Next, while the students wait outside the classroom door, enter the room, sit at a table, and pretend to eat something from a bowl. Students enter the room one at a time, approach the table where you're sitting, stop, say their lines, and then walk to the back of the room.)

Dialogue Play

Student 1: Oh! (*Surprised. He's surprised he's come upon someone eating.*)

Student 2: What? (*Questioning. He wonders what's in the bowl.*)

Student 3: No! (*Disbelief. He can't believe he's seeing what he's seeing.*)

Student 4: Yikes! (*Frightened. She thinks she may have to eat some, too.*)

Student 5: Hmmm. (*Wondering. She wonders if the food combination tastes good.*)

Student 6: Hey! (*Somewhat angry. He was planning to eat that bowl of food!*)

Student 7: Why? (*Questioning. He wonders why anyone would eat such a combination.*)

Student 8: Well? (*Questioning. He wonders if the person likes the food.*)

Student 9: Ugh! (*Disgusted. He is grossed out by the food combination.*)

Teacher: Sauerkraut and Pudding! (*Happily.*)

☀ After the play is done, read aloud the story you've chosen for modeling. Have students create their own dialogue plays. Tell students to use one-word lines, as you and the students did in the sample dialogue play. You may want to list possible words on the board (see Teacher Tip). Students should work in pairs or small groups.

☀ Stress to students that, like the sample dialogue play, their dialogue play must tell a story. After students perform their play, ask audience members to explain what was going on. Invite them to suggest changes for clarity.

On Their Own

Provide students with a copy of page 96. Have them work in pairs or small groups to write dialogue plays based on the book or story they've read. Encourage students to perform their dialogues for the class.

> **TEACHER TIP**
>
> *Provide students with a list of words such as: oh, what, yikes, ummm, hey, why, well, ugh, where, when, yes, no, them, this, that, good, me she, us, so, go, how, her, and it.*

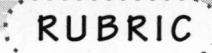
Dialogue Play

Name_____ Date_____

Story/Book Title _____

Author_____

Category	Excellent	Above Average	Average	Below Average
Clarity of meaning	Clearly focused; completely understandable	Clear meaning throughout	At times a bit confusing	Confusing in many places
Effort/ attitude	Enthusiastic	Appropriate	Adequate	Apathetic
Word choice	Dynamic word choice	Outstanding word choice	Appropriate word choice	Awkward word choice
Significance of events mentioned in dialogue	Most vital events mentioned in dialogue	Significant events mentioned in dialogue	Some events important	Unimportant events mentioned

Teacher's Comments: _____

_____

_____

_____

_____

_____

_____

_____